Contents

AF270788

Welcome to PineCar Racing

PineCar Racers® are small, model racecars, built to specific dimensions and raced by gravity down an inclined track. PineCar Racing is an all-round wholesome activity, and derby races are events sponsored and organized by all sorts of groups. The Boy Scouts of America®, Kub Kar™, Royal Racers®, Awana™ and other scouting organizations sponsor races annually. Church groups, summer camps, businesses and other groups also sponsor races for fun, team building and fundraising activities.

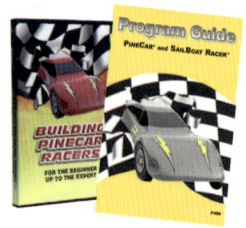

Building a racer is a source of enjoyment, learning and skill building. Parents and children also benefit from the time they spend together designing and building a car. This book is a learning tool that offers you step-by-step instruction to guide you in designing and building the car you want. You will learn the tips and techniques you need to turn a simple block of wood into a finished, sleek, fast-running racer.

PineCar also offers an instructional video, **Building PineCar Racers** in DVD (P3941) or VHS (P3940) that includes tips and techniques on building, painting, customizing, adding accessories and racing PineCar or **SailBoat Racers**®. The **PineCar Race Package** (P459) includes a 32-foot regulation track and the supplies you need to hold a race. The **Program Guide** (P450) provides complete instruction on how to sponsor and organize a race. You can also access dozens of videos on the PineCar.com website about designing your car, making speed modifications and customizing its look.

Before You Start

Your first step in the planning and building process is to become fully informed on your local race rules. Sometimes awards are given for both speed and craftsmanship. Race rules will often differ in regards to racer length, width and weight specifications. They can also vary in the preparations and/or modifications they allow to wheels and axles. You also want to check to see the type of lubricants they allow participants to use.

We have included the most commonly used racing specifications and rules, however each derby race is different, and the derby organizers should provide a copy of their specific race rules to the participants.

Next, it is very important that you read this entire book before beginning to build your car. You might also consider watching some of the how-to videos offered on the PineCar website to help you plan ahead. It takes time to have a good looking and speedy racer. Researching the process before you start will save you time and make your experience of building a racer more fun and satisfying. As you read, it is a good idea to make notes on the tools and materials you have available and those you will need to gather and/or purchase before you design, cut, build and decorate your car.

The PineCar products mentioned in this book are referenced with a page number, which leads you to the Product Listing section in the back of the book. This section is meant to present a complete list of the PineCar products available to build your car. Most or all of these are available at your local hobby shop or hardware store.

If you have been provided a racer kit, read the instructions completely and examine the contents of the kit. As you continue through this book, we will discuss the designing and cutting of your racer depending on whether you have a block or a pre-cut racer body. If you still have to purchase a kit, this book will help you make the correct choice depending on the equipment available to you and your skill level.

Throughout this how-to book, you will find **Tricked-out for Speed**. Speed tricks are for serious racers who are looking for a winning edge. These tricks are based on the scientific principles that make a car fast. Maximize your car's potential energy and reduce friction as much as possible. Verify race rules before applying these techniques.

You will also find **Go Above & Beyond**. The steps involve using PineCar **Precision Tools** (pg. 56). These high-end tools are CNC machined and designed explicitly to correct standard manufacturing imperfections of mass-produced car bodies, axles and wheels. They will also help to fine-tune a racer for optimum performance and speed. Verify race rules before using Precision Tools.

Building a winning PineCar Racer® is not a last minute task, it takes time and preparation. The more time you devote to your car, the better it will look and the faster it will go. Every step is important and each shaves time off your car's performance.

GENERAL RACING SPECIFICATIONS

Always refer to your local race rules. Cars that do not meet racing specifications may be disqualified. It is also a good idea to check the official district rules in case you advance from your local derby. The same race rules do not always apply.

1. Maximum racer size (including wheels) may not exceed 7" in length and 2-3/4" in width.

2. Minimum width between wheels is 1-3/4".

3. Minimum clearance between racer bottom and track is 3/8".

4. Maximum weight of racer may not exceed 5 oz.

5. No wheel bearings, washers and bushings are allowed. Racer shall not ride on any type of springs. Loose, liquid or moving materials are strictly prohibited.

6. The racer may be built up to the maximum weight allowed by adding wood or metal, provided the additional material is securely built into the racer body.

7. Decorative details are permissible as long as they do not exceed the maximum length, width and weight specifications.

8. Racer must be freewheeling. Starting devices are forbidden.

9. Axle type should be the same on all racers.

Plan and Design Your Racer

Designing your car from a simple block of wood will be one of the most rewarding steps in building your gravity-driven racer. Take your time, plan out your design and be creative. Some of the more popular styles are Grand Prix racers, roadsters, funny cars, trucks and dragsters. You can get ideas from car magazines, books and websites. Keep in mind what tools you have available, your skill level, and the amount of time you have to complete the car.

When designing a racer that is built for speed, there are elements that must be taken into consideration when planning your car's design. These elements include center of gravity, wind resistance and weight distribution. These principles set the foundation for a winning car.

CENTER OF GRAVITY

Center of Gravity (CoG) is the balancing point of an object. For a PineCar Racer, a CoG near the rear of the car maximizes its potential energy. When a gravity-driven car runs on a sloped racetrack, the rear of the car sets higher and travels downhill for a longer distance than the front. Placing most of the racer's weight in the rear produces more potential energy. When the car is in motion, potential energy is converted into kinetic energy, and the additional kinetic energy will give your racer a push to the finish line.

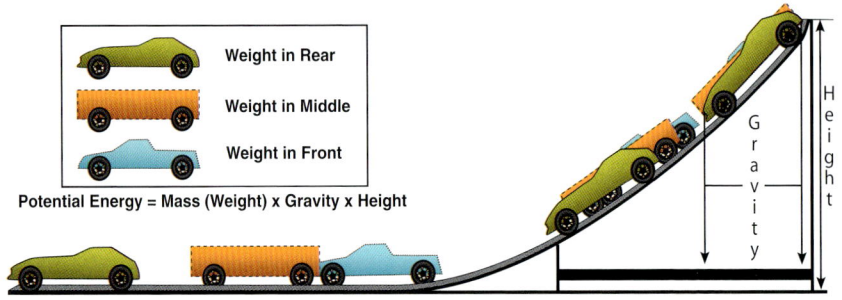

Potential Energy = Mass (Weight) x Gravity x Height

Potential Energy
Potential energy is the amount of energy stored in an object due to the variables, mass x gravity x height. It is called potential energy because it has the "potential" to be converted into kinetic energy.

Kinetic Energy
Kinetic Energy is the amount of energy an object has while in motion.

Center Of Gravity (CoG)
Center of Gravity is the balancing point of an object.

6

OPTIMUM COG

Finding the optimum CoG location for your racer will ensure ultimate speed and stability. As stated, a CoG near the rear of the car creates additional potential energy. However, if the CoG is too far to the rear, the car will be unstable traveling down the track. A good starting point for determining optimum CoG for your racer is 3/4" in front of the rear axle.

TRACK TYPE

Some experts believe track type plays an important role in determining the best CoG for a car.

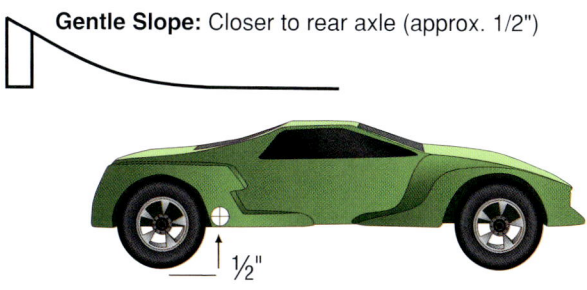

Gentle Slope: Closer to rear axle (approx. 1/2")

½"

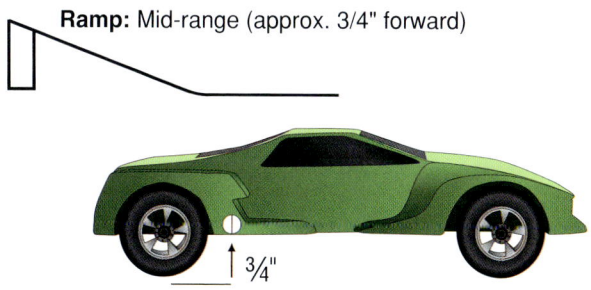

Ramp: Mid-range (approx. 3/4" forward)

¾"

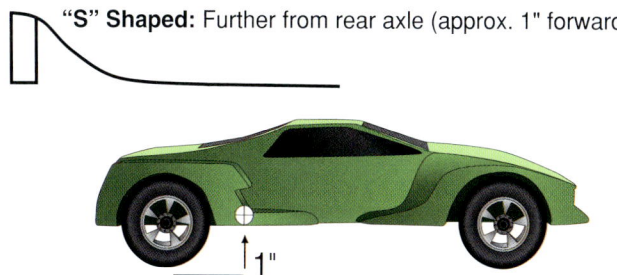

"S" Shaped: Further from rear axle (approx. 1" forward)

1"

TIP! If the track type is unknown, set CoG at 3/4" in front of the rear axle.

AERODYNAMICS

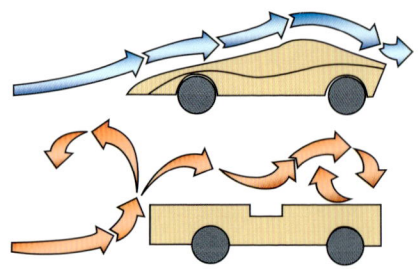

A racer with an aerodynamic design has less wind resistance because the air is allowed to move over and around the car body. With all factors being equal, the car with a lean, contoured design is faster. Squared fronts may cause turbulence rather than allowing air to flow freely. A thin, aerodynamic design also gives you more control over weight distribution.

When designing a thin racer, be sure to leave enough wood for the type of weight you plan to use.

REAR-WEIGHTED

The weighted portion of a gravity-driven car continues to accelerate until it reaches the flat area of track. Therefore, a front-weighted car will start to slow down before a rear-weighted car. On rear-weighted designs, the back of the car sets higher and drops further than the front and the effect is observable. It will appear as if the car received a push toward the finish line. There are a lot of style options when designing a rear-weighted car. For instance, a very thin body **(Fig. 1)** allows for precision weight placement and a wedge-shaped car **(Fig. 2)** by design has most of the weight in the back.

Thin Body **Fig. 1**

Wedge **Fig. 2**

What Else You Can Do...

Build two racers and race them against each other. Focus on the slower racer. Make weight placement modifications and adjustment until the slower car becomes the faster of the two. Repeat this process until you are happy with the speed of one of the racers.

Lay Out Your Design

MAKE A TEMPLATE

If you are not sure how to cut out your block to form your desired car shape, we recommend using a template. You can either purchase a template or make your own.

Begin by positioning your wood block on its side on a piece of paper. Trace around the block with a pencil, taking care to mark the axle slots **(Fig. 3)**. Label this Side View. Next, place the block top-side up, trace around the bottom edge and mark the axle slots **(Fig. 4)**. Label this Top View **(Fig. 5)**.

As you are designing your racer, it is important to not exceed the maximum dimensions allowed per official race rules. On the tracings, use a ruler to mark dotted lines to show the maximum width and length dimensions allowed **(Fig. 6)**.

Set a pair of your official racing wheels over the axle notches on the Side View tracing. Make sure they are centered and positioned properly, then trace around them. Trace wheels onto the Top View also **(Fig. 6)**. If you have access to a copy machine, make several copies of your tracings so you can try different variations of your design ideas.

Now that you have the wood block traced and the maximum dimensions marked, lay out your design **(Fig. 7)**. It is easier to draw the Side View first, then the Top View. Be creative and try modifying a few lines on the tracings.

Plan for the placement of details such as decals, engines, roll bars, canopies, drivers or other custom parts. Use your imagination and have fun!

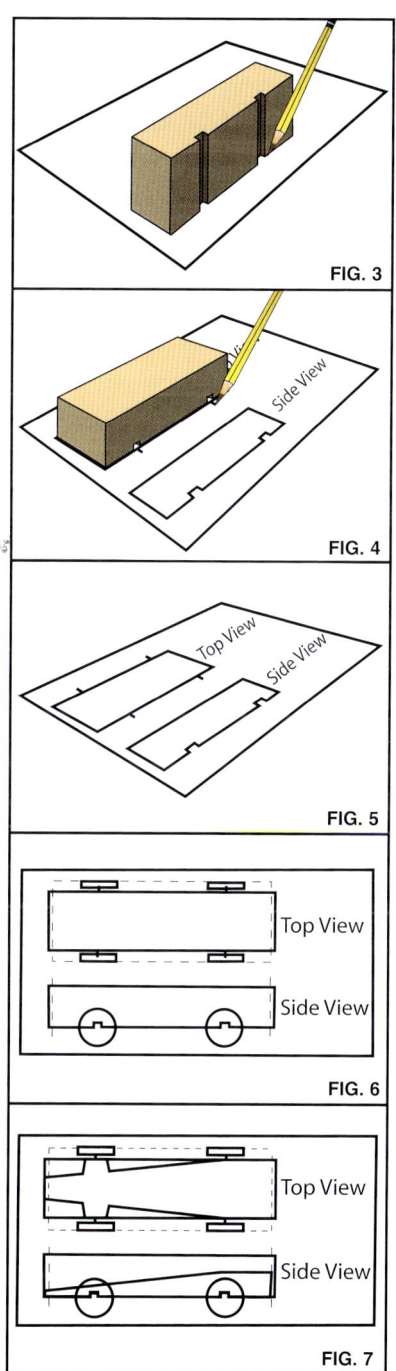

FIG. 3

FIG. 4

FIG. 5

Top View

Side View

FIG. 6

Top View

Side View

FIG. 7

CHOOSE WEIGHTS

Deciding on the type of weight to use and the perfect location to place them is one of the biggest factors in building a winning car. Because derby racers use only gravity to propel them, you want your racer to weigh the maximum amount allowed per race rules.

WEIGHT PLACEMENT

As explained in the Center of Gravity section (pg. 6), the weighted portion of a gravity-driven car continues to accelerate until it reaches the flat area of track. Therefore, a rear-weighted car will continue to accelerate longer than a front-weighted car. Weights should be initially positioned as far to the rear of the car as possible, but allow yourself the ability to move them forward when testing for your racer's optimum center of gravity. This will be covered in *Make Your Car Race Ready*, page 36.

WEIGHT CHOICES

PineCar has a wide range of weight choices to accommodate any level of racing. Weights are available in various styles and shapes to meet your racer's needs. There are aerodynamic, tungsten and incremental weights. Choosing the best weight for your racer depends on a variety of factors. Ask yourself, do you want a weight that enriches the design of your car (Chassis Weight, pg. 55), allows for easy weight modifications (Incremental, pg. 54-55) or gives you the ability to pin-point weight placement (Tungsten, pg. 55)?

Lead-Free Weights

Made of lead-free alloy, weights include **Incremental, Aerodynamic** and **Chassis** styles **(Fig. 8, 9 and 10)**. These weights are mounted onto the bottom, sides or top of your racer, or inserted into a predrilled cavity. For easy weight adjustments, incremental weights are scored to allow you to break off sections with pliers **(Fig. 11)** or cut with a coping saw.

FIG. 8

FIG. 9

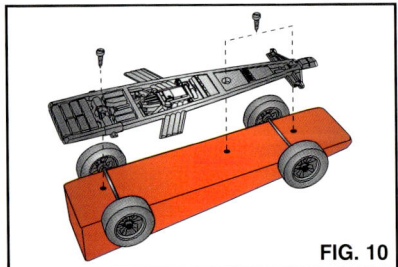

FIG. 10

FIG. 11

Tungsten Lead-Free Weights

Tungsten Incremental Weights give you ultimate control over precise weight placement. They are 1.7 times denser than lead and nearly three times as dense as traditional weights. This allows you to place more weight in a small, precise area, making it easier to fine-tune the center of gravity (CoG) and ideal for racers with a thin body design. Their incremental design allows you to weight your racer in exact 1/16 (0.0625) ounce increments. Available in cylinder **(Fig. 12)** and plate **(Fig. 13)** styles.

FIG. 12

FIG. 13

Tungsten CoG Weights (Fig. 14)

Fine-tune your car's CoG. The unique, interlocking-threaded design makes weight adjustments easy. Reposition forward or backward, without cross-threading.

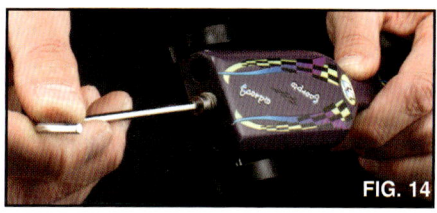
FIG. 14

Key & Groove

EZ-Cut Tungsten Weights (Fig. 15)

A cylindrical tungsten weight that is easy to cut, carve and sand to achieve precise weight requirements.

FIG. 15

Tungsten Putty Weight (Fig. 16)

Use for last minute weight modifications. It is easy to mold and shape, and is non-hardening.

FIG. 16

AXLE SLOTS

Before cutting out your racer, verify the axle slots are at a 90° angle to the wood block. PineCar offers the **Wheel Alignment Tool** (pg. 53) to check alignment **(Fig. 17)**. When axle slots are not perpendicular to the wood block, consider using the **Axle Slot Jig** (pg. 56) to correct the flaws (this tool is for use with nail-type axles only).

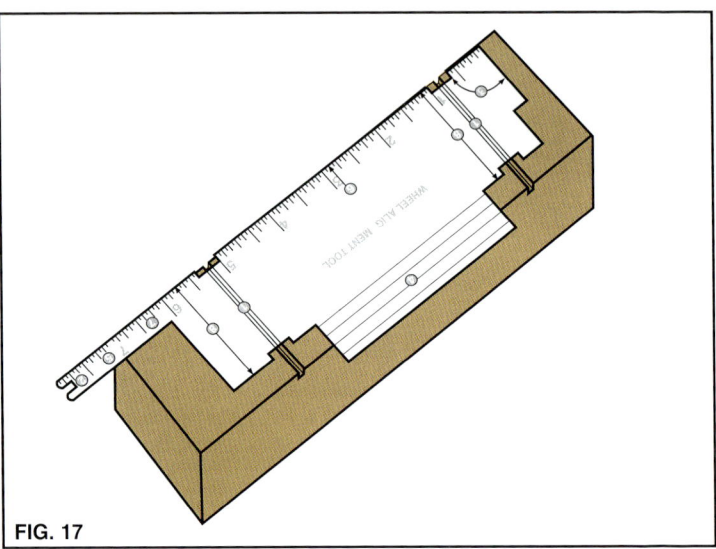

FIG. 17

CHOOSE A SAW

Choose a saw that best fits your skill level. No matter what type of saw you use, be sure the blade is sharp and you wear eye protection. Many saw accidents occur because people use dull blades. The most important point we can make is *Safety Comes First* and adult supervision is always recommended. Remember, this is typically an adult/child project. When choosing a saw, we suggest using the **Racer Shaping Tools** (pg. 56).

ROUGH CUT YOUR RACER

- After you have selected your racer design, cut out your template tracings.
- Place the Side View template on one side of the block, lining up the axle slots. Holding the paper firmly in place, trace around the template with a pencil **(Fig. 18)**. When using a coping saw, trace the template on both sides of the block to help maintain an even cut.
- Place the block in a vise (do not over tighten) and cut out the side view design **(Fig. 19)**.

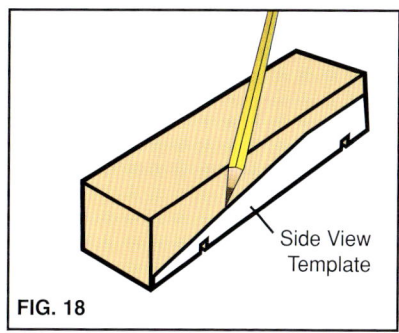

FIG. 18

FIG. 19

• Place the Top View template on top of the racer and trace around it **(Fig. 20)**. If the top of your racer is contoured, your template may have to be cut to lie flat. Cut out the top view design **(Fig. 21)**.

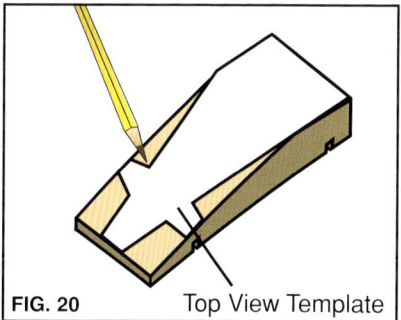

FIG. 20   Top View Template

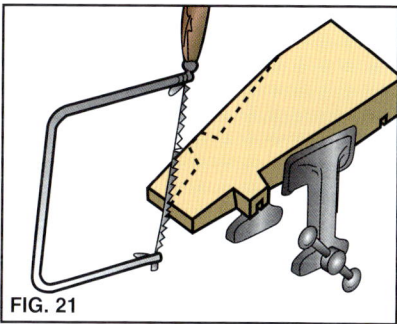

FIG. 21

CUT WEIGHT CAVITY

Installation of weights will vary depending on weight type. For example, **Round Incremental Weights** (pg. 54) are installed into a 3/8" diameter cavity **(Fig. 22 and 23)**. Detailed weight installation instructions are included with all PineCar weights.

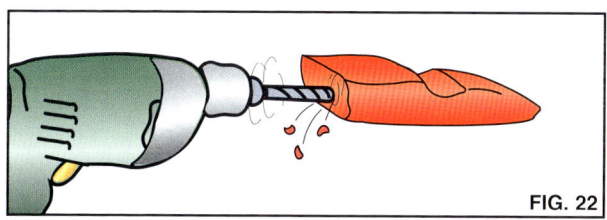

FIG. 22

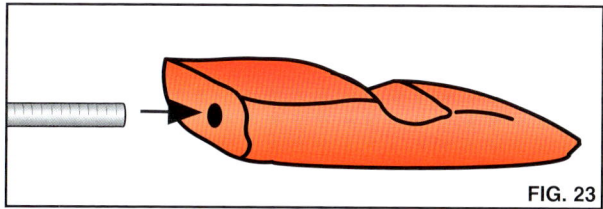

FIG. 23

13

PRE-CUT DESIGNS

If you do not have woodworking skills or the tools needed to design and cut a racer, PineCar has a large selection of **Pre-Cut Designs** (pg. 42-43). There are basic and full body designs in popular styles, aerodynamic designs, low-profile designs and a basic wedge shape. They are rough-cut and ready to finish. The **Aerodynamic Pre-Cut Designs** have predrilled weight cavities, and standard and extended wheelbases.

WOOD DETAILS

When using scrap pieces of wood or the **Body Builder Kit** (pg. 43) to make added details for your racer, such as fenders, fins, spoilers, pipes, canopies or other body details, now is the time to cut them out **(Fig. 24)**.

FIG. 24

WHAT ELSE YOU CAN DO...

MOVE COG TOWARD REAR OF CAR

If your racer design is front-heavy, such as a truck, you can modify the racer body to make it rear-weighted.

- Drill out wood from underneath the racer in the center of the body **(Fig. 25 and 26)**. This will allow more weight to be placed near the rear of the car.

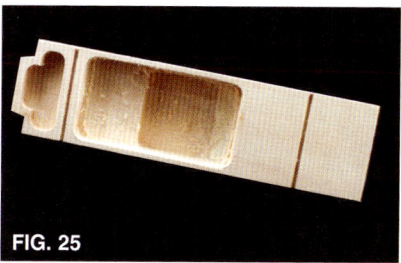
FIG. 25

- To ensure you do not drill through the car body, wrap masking tape around a 1/4" drill bit at the depth that you want to drill **(Fig. 27)**.

- Use a fulcrum point or edge of a pencil to verify preliminary center of gravity **(Fig. 28)**. It should be off-center, toward the rear axles.

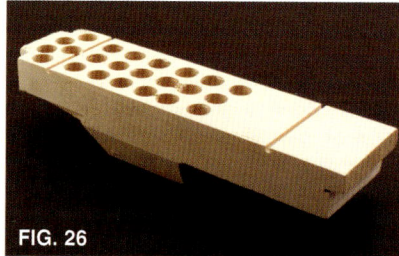
FIG. 26

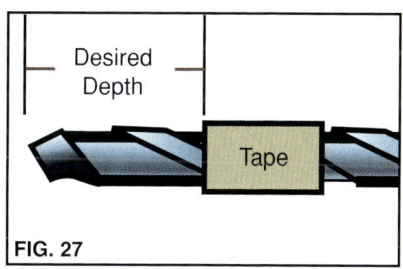

Desired
Depth

Tape

FIG. 27

FIG. 28

HIDDEN WEIGHT CAVITY

Predrill a hidden weight cavity in case your car weighs-in light on race day. It is easy to add additional weight with **Tungsten Putty Weight** (pg. 55).

- On the underside of your car, drill a 1/4" diameter hole, 3/16" deep. It should be centered and toward the rear **(Fig. 29)**.

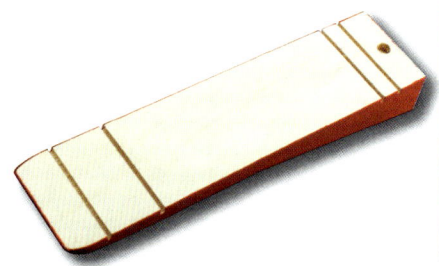

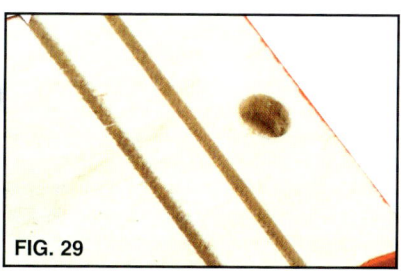
FIG. 29

TRICKED-OUT FOR SPEED

Check official race rules before executing.

EXTENDED WHEELBASE

An extended wheelbase gives your racer a two-fold speed advantage. First, it allows your car to travel in a straight line down the track. Traveling in a straight line will limit the amount of times the car bumps into the center guide. Fewer bumps mean more speed.

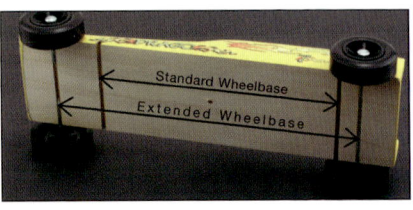

Second, it allows weight to be placed even further toward the rear of the car.

Here are two methods for making an extended wheelbase.

Drill New Axle Holes

Use the **Axle Slot Jig** (pg. 56) to drill new axle holes approximately 5/8" from both ends and 1/8" from bottom **(Fig. 30)**. It includes complete instructions on how to drill new holes. For use with nail-type axles only

FIG. 30

Cut New Axle Grooves

Practice on a piece of scrap wood before modifying your racer.

Mark Grooves

• Begin by marking position of new grooves with a ruler and sharp pencil. Make a number of short marks 16 mm from the front end of the car. Draw a straight line across the block connecting the marks **(Fig. 31)**.

FIG. 31

• Make a second set of marks 2 mm from first line (toward the center of the car) **(Fig. 32)**. Draw a straight line across the marks. This is the width of the groove.

• Repeat these steps on the back end of the car **(Fig. 33)**.

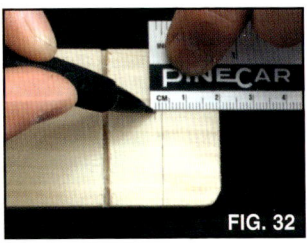

FIG. 32

• On the side of the block in the center of the new groove lines, mark 2.5 mm down. This will be the depth of the axle slots **(Fig. 34)**.

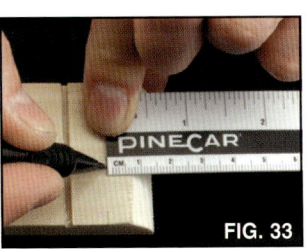

FIG. 33

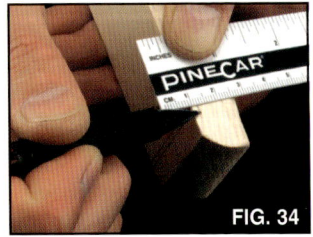

FIG. 34

Cut Grooves

• Place car in a vise. Do not over tighten.

• Use a coping saw to cut grooves. Starting with the front of the car, place saw blade just inside the first line with the blade at a 45-degree angle. Draw the blade down slowly, cutting into the wood with light pressure **(Fig. 35)**.

• Pivot blade forward until the saw is level with the surface of the car. Keep your cuts straight and parallel with the pencil line. Make the cuts short with light pressure. You will get more accurate cuts and better control of the blade path if you use only the first third of the blade closest to the handle. Continue until you reach a level depth of 2.5 mm **(Fig. 36)**.

• Repeat, cutting just inside the second line. This will complete the first extended groove on the front of the car.

• Repeat procedure to cut groove on back end of car.

• Verify grooves are perpendicular to car body using the **Wheel Alignment Tool** (pg. 53).

FIG. 35

FIG. 36

THREE-WHEEL RIDING

As you get further into this book, you will learn friction is the enemy of speed! A friction reducing trick is to raise one of the front wheels off the track, so your racer rides on three wheels instead of four **(Fig. 37)**. Use **Axle Slot Jig** (pg. 56) to drill a raised axle slot.

For an alternative **Three-Wheel Riding** technique, see page 31.

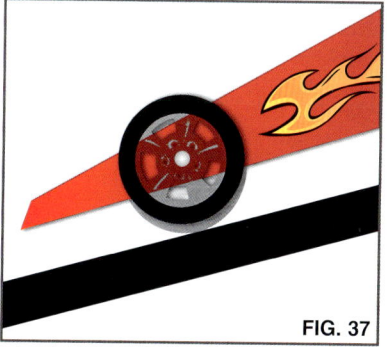

FIG. 37

Shape, Sand and Paint

SHAPE AND SAND

Shaping and sanding your racer is very important to the finished look. Notice that racecars have rounded corners. Rounded corners give a more aerodynamic shape, which helps reduce wind resistance and friction.

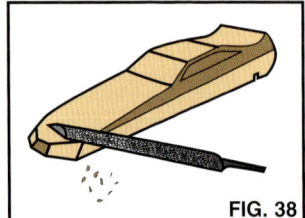

FIG. 38

When shaping your racer, you will need a wood rasp (coarse file with cutting teeth, which is included with the **Racer Shaping Tools**) and sandpaper. We suggest sanding against the grain when removing large amounts of wood, but do not press too hard or you may damage your racer. Start shaping with a rasp **(Fig. 38)** to smooth overly rough spots and round edges you want to contour.

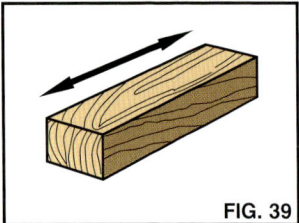

FIG. 39

After the shaping is complete, sand your car with coarse-grade sandpaper. When sanding, follow the direction of the grain **(Fig. 39)**. Sanding cross-grain may produce a rough surface. Sand until the rough shaping marks are gone. Next, use medium-grade sandpaper to remove the marks caused by the coarse sandpaper. Finally, sand with fine-grade sandpaper until the surface is completely smooth.

Wipe car with a clean, soft cloth to remove dust. **TIP!** For sanding hard-to-reach areas, glue a small piece of sandpaper to the end of a craft stick, or use an emery board.

SEAL AND PAINT

SEAL RACER BODY

Cover your racer in **Body Putty** (pg. 56) or wood filler to hide pits, dents and scratches. Apply the putty, allow it to dry and sand with fine-grade sandpaper. Apply **Sanding Sealer** (pg. 50) before painting to fill in the wood grain and create a smooth, aerodynamic finish.

CHOOSE TYPE OF PAINT

When choosing the type of paint to use, there are different factors to consider. Read manufacturers' labels for cleanup instructions, drying times, thinners and toxicity. You can either brush or spray paint onto your racer. The **Complete Paint System** or a **Custom Finishing Kit** (pg. 50) contains sealer/paint. The paint seals the wood, so a separate sanding sealer is not required. The following information can help you decide the type of paint to use.

Brush-on Paint

- We recommend water-based paint for younger modelers. It cleans up easily, dries faster, is non-toxic, non-flammable and can be thinned with water.
- A soft bristle or foam brush (approximately 1" wide) will be best for painting a racer.
- If a primer is recommended, apply two to three coats and allow each coat to dry thoroughly. Sand lightly between coats. **NOTE:** Oil-based primer may take up to 24 hours to dry.
- Apply two to three coats of paint. Allow each coat to dry thoroughly. Sand lightly between coats. Do not sand after final coat of paint.

Spray Paint

- A fast-drying enamel usually gives the best results.
- Apply two to three coats of primer, sanding lightly between coats. The primer will provide a smooth surface for the spray paint. Hold the can 12-16" from the racer when spraying. If you are too close, the paint will run. If you are too far away, the paint will dry before it hits the surface, causing a dust-like effect.
- When using spray paint, be certain to cover the entire work area with newspapers. Spray paint covers a large area and can be very messy. Apply two to three coats of paint, lightly sanding between coats. Make sure the paint is completely dry before sanding or it will gum up on your sandpaper. It may take as long as 24-hours to dry between coats. Do not sand after the final coat.

Painting Tips

- Pick a dust-free environment to paint in and cover the entire area with newspapers for easy cleanup. Wipe the surface of your racer with a soft, clean cloth before each coat of paint. Clean the brush with the appropriate cleaner after each coat. Do not let paint dry on the brush.
- Make a paint stand. Drive three nails through a block of wood **(Fig. 40)**.
- When using two different colors to paint your racer, use painter's tape or masking tape to mask the areas you do not want painted a certain color.
- Cover the area you do not want painted with tape **(Fig. 41)**. Paint the first color and let it dry completely and then remove the tape.
- Apply tape onto the painted area. If you apply the tape before the paint is completely dry, it will remove some of the

FIG. 40

Tape

Tape

FIG. 41

paint. Paint the rest of the car. After the final coat of paint is dry, remove the masking tape.

WHAT ELSE YOU CAN DO...

As a paint alternative, cover your racer with a **Body Skin Custom Transfer** (pg. 45). They are a great way to customize your racer, while making it look sleek and stylish.

GLOSS/WAX FINISH

After you have painted your racer, you may want to apply a high-gloss finish to protect your paint job and add a shiny finish. We recommend a brush-on, water-based gloss. A gloss finish is included in all the PineCar paint kits. It provides a shiny finish if you have used a flat paint. **PineCar Wax** (pg. 50) provides an allover shine.

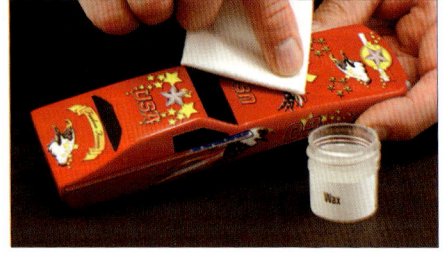

DETAILS AND DECALS

Detail pieces are pipes, headers, decals, canopies, windshields, fenders, etc. You may have already made details out of wood or you can create them from a multitude of household items. PineCar has loads of **Custom Parts** (pg. 51-52) and **Dry Transfer Decals** (pg. 46-49) to add personality to any racer **(Fig. 42)**. Some details will be added before painting and some will be added afterward. Refer to package instructions for information. Remember to keep the weight, width and length of the racer a priority when adding details!

Your racer should now have its final look. You have designed, cut out, painted, added details and applied a gloss finish.

FIG. 42

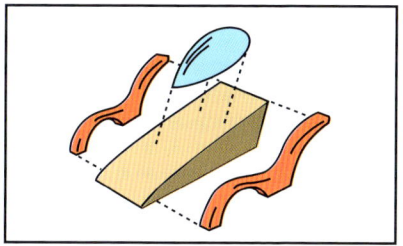

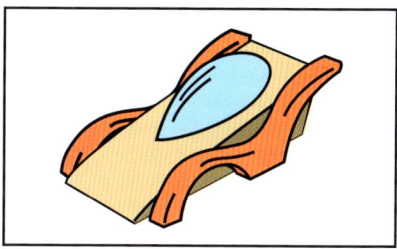

Prepare Axles

AXLE TYPES

One-piece

Nail-type

One of the most important factors for building a fast car is reducing friction. The more friction your racer produces, the slower it will go. One of the main sources of friction is the contact between the wheels and axles. Wheels spin faster on axles that are polished to a mirror-like shine. **TIP!** Avoid last minute problems and prepare a few extra wheels and axles, just in case.

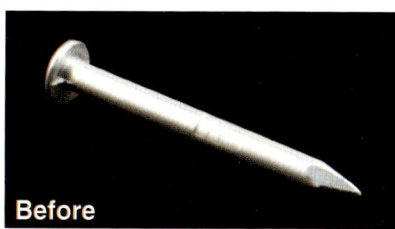

Before

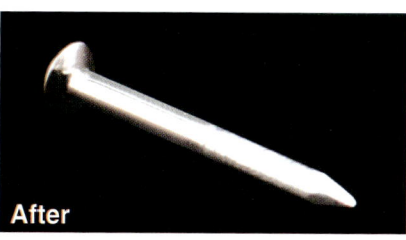

After

SUGGESTED TOOLS AND MATERIALS

- Variable Speed Electric Drill (not to exceed 1,200 RPM, follow manufacturer's safety recommendations)
- Table Vice
- Polishing Pumice◊ or Wet/Dry Polishing Paper (Grits: #400, 600, 800, 1000, 1200, 1500 and 2000)*
- Triangular File*
- Magnifying Glass*
- Safety Glasses
- Dish of Water

◊Included with Axles & Polishing Kit (P359)
*Included with Micro-Polishing System (P4038)

ONE-PIECE AXLES

One-piece axles do not have burrs to remove, but they should be polished to reduce friction. See Polish Axles with Pumice or Progressive Polish Axles on page 23 and 24 for instructions on how to polish axles.

NAIL-TYPE AXLES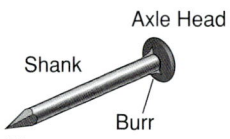

To have a competitive edge, burrs need to be removed and axles must be polished. It is crucial to not skip these steps.

Axle Head

Shank

Burr

Tip

FILE AXLE TIP

The edges of the axle tip can damage the inside of the wheel hub.

- Use a file to smooth the sharp edges of axle tips **(Fig. 43)**.

REMOVE BURRS

Due to the molding process, axles have burrs. Burrs create a huge amount of friction against the wheel hub.

- Clamp drill in a padded vice. Secure pointed end of axle in drill check, leaving 3/8" exposed.

- Run drill at medium speed. Hold the flat side of a triangle file to the underside of the axle head and along shank **(Fig. 44)**. Move file in a slight back-and-forth motion for a few seconds. Do NOT over file and weaken the axle.

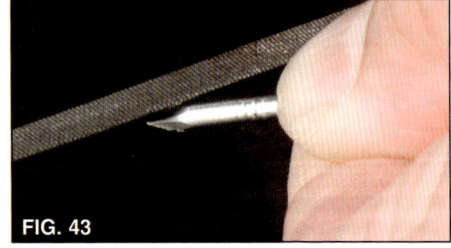

FIG. 43

FIG. 44

Shape Axles

Use the **Axle Shaper** (pg. 56) to reduce friction by straightening and rounding the axle shank and squaring the axle head to the shank. Axles that are not aligned properly cause wheels to wobble, which will slow down your car.

POLISH AXLES

Here are two methods for polishing axles.

Polish Axles with Pumice

Polish axles with pumice to remove rough spots and pits on the shank and improve the performance of your racer by providing shiny, smooth axles. Use the **Axles & Polishing Kit** (pg. 53) for polishing with pumice.

• Clamp drill in padded vice. Secure pointed end of axle in drill chuck, leaving 3/8" exposed.

• Dip a 1/4" x 4" strip of #600-grit wet/dry sandpaper in water. Hold ends of strip and apply to axle shank. Pass back and forth for 10-15 seconds **(Fig. 45)**. Turn off drill, wipe axle clean. Repeat, if necessary.

• Mix a small amount of pumice with water (oatmeal consistency). Place a drop of mixture in the center of a 1/4" x 4" strip of soft cloth. Run drill at medium speed and pass strip back and forth until the axle shines.

FIG. 45

Progressive Polish Axles

To ensure the slickest wheel spin, we recommend progressively polishing axles with seven different grits of wet/dry polishing paper: #400, 600, 800, 1000, 1200, 1500 and 2000. Use the **Micro-Polishing System** (pg. 54) for progressive polishing.

- Cut a strip 1/4" wide x 4-1/2" long from each of the seven grits. Write the grit number on back of each strip to avoid confusion. Each strip of polishing paper should polish two axles.
- Clamp drill in a padded vice. Secure pointed end of axle in drill chuck, leaving 3/8" exposed.
- Run drill at medium speed. Dip a strip of #400-grit polishing paper in water. Hold ends of strip and apply coarse side to axle shank and pass back and forth for about 10-15 seconds **(Fig. 45)**. Then, polish under axle head. Turn off drill, wipe axle clean.
- Monitor polishing progress with a magnifying glass. If there are any deep scratches or rough areas remaining, polish again.
- Repeat procedure with each grit of polishing paper, working from coarsest to finest grade. Extend polishing time by 5 seconds for each grit. i.e. #400 (10-15 seconds), #600 (15-20 seconds), #800 (20-25 seconds), etc. **NOTE:** The higher the grit number, the finer the grade.
- For a sleek look, progressively polish each axle head **(Fig. 46)**.

FIG. 46

Finish Axles after a Progressive Polish

To take polishing to the next level and reduce friction even further, we recommend using the **Diamond Finishing Kit** (pg. 54) after a progressive polish. It precision-polishes axles and wheel hubs to virtually eliminate friction. The included **Diamond Compound** is equivalent to a #8000-grit polishing cloth.

TRICKED-OUT FOR SPEED

Reduce friction even further! Be sure to check your official race rules before executing. **These tricks should be done prior to polishing axles.**

CHAMFER AXLE HEAD

Chamfering creates a beveled edge on the head of nail-type axles, reducing the contact area between the axle head and the outside of the wheel hub. This can be done easily with the **Axle Shaper** (pg. 56), or use a drill and triangular file.

Beveled Edge

• Clamp drill in a padded vice. Secure the pointed end of an axle in drill chuck, leaving 3/8" exposed **(Fig. 47)**.

• Run drill at medium speed. Lay flat side of a triangular file against backside of axle head. Tilt the file forward and gently file the axle head to an angle of approximately 30 degrees **(Fig. 48)**. When finished, the axle head will have a slight bowed appearance. **IMPORTANT:** Do NOT apply heavy downward pressure on axle.

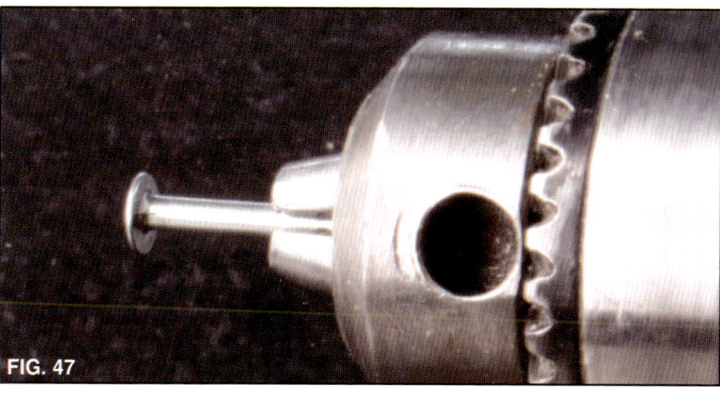

FIG. 47

FIG. 48

NOTCH AXLE SHANK

Reduce the contact area between wheel hub and axle by filing a 1/8" wide notch in the axle shank. Less contact area means less friction! The notch also acts as a secret compartment for holding extra lubricant.

- Clamp drill in a padded vice. Secure pointed end of axle in drill chuck, leaving 3/8" exposed.

- Make a mark on the axle shank, 1/8" from the axle head **(Fig. 49)**. Place a second mark 1/8" from first mark **(Fig. 50)**.

- Run drill at medium speed. Place 1/8" triangular file on the axle, in between marked areas **(Fig. 51)**. File to a depth of approximately 1/64" **(Fig. 52)**. Do not cut the notch too deep or it will weaken the axle. Repeat for each axle.

FIG. 49

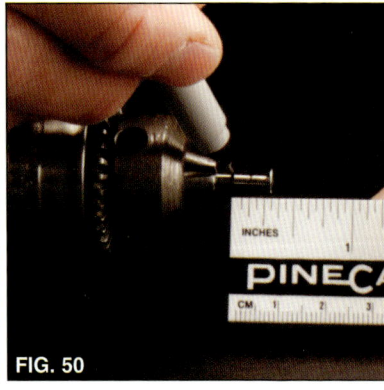

FIG. 50

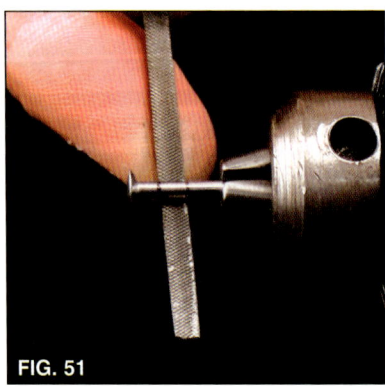

FIG. 51

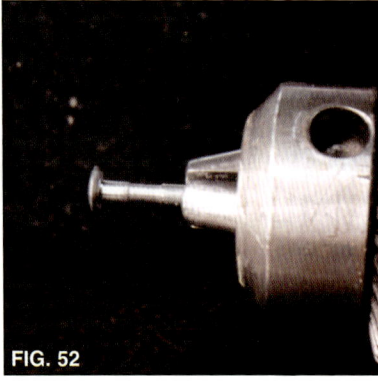

FIG. 52

GO ABOVE AND BEYOND

Bend axles using the **Straight Tracker** and **Axle Shaper** (pg. 56). Bending axles is beneficial in a number of ways. It provides precision alignment and can be used to implement the **Rail Riding**™ technique.

PRECISION ALIGNMENT

Optimize your car's performance by bending axles for precision alignment. This will ensure your car travels in a straight line, down the entire length of track.

RAIL RIDING

Rail Riding uses the front dominant wheel to gently steer the car into the track guide for the duration of the race **(Fig. 53)**. This technique is beneficial because it keeps the racer from bumping into and off of the track guide. When a car bumps the track guide, it causes the car to change direction and bump into the guide on the other side. These impacts cause a breaking effect and slow down the racer. It also increases the distance traveled down the track.
TIP! Some experts believe, precision aligning rear wheels, Three-Wheel Riding and Rail Riding are key to having the fastest car on the track.

CANTED WHEELS

Bend rear axles to cant rear wheels so they run on their inside edges and reduce friction **(Fig. 54)**.

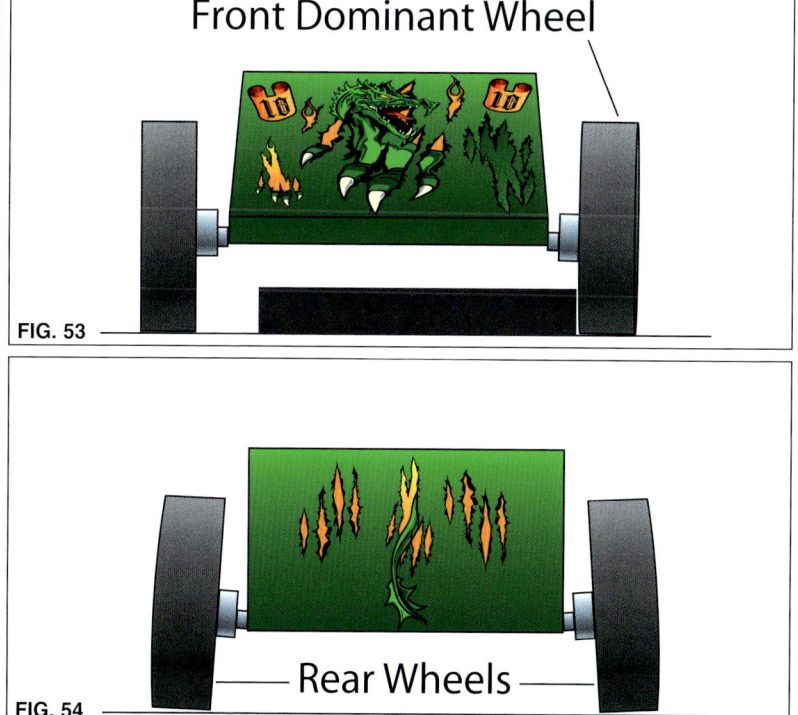

Front Dominant Wheel

FIG. 53

Rear Wheels

FIG. 54

Wheels

Tuned wheels are essential for a fast, winning racer. Wheels have blemishes due to the molding process. If these blemishes are left as is, they will create friction and greatly reduce the speed of your car. Wheels must be sanded lightly and tuned before they are attached to your racer.

Suggested Tools and Materials

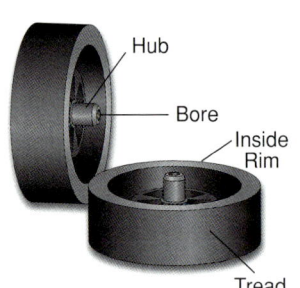
Hub
Bore
Inside Rim
Tread

- Variable Speed Electric Drill (not to exceed 1,200 RPM, follow manufacturer's safety recommendations)
- Table Vice
- Safety Glasses
- Wheel Turning Mandrel (pg. 53)
- 1/8" Triangular File*
- 2 Grades of Sandpaper (fine and medium)
- 3 Grits of Wet/Dry Polishing Paper (#400, 600, 1000)*
- Magnifying Glass*
- Dish of Water
  *Materials included with Micro-Polishing System (P4038).

GO ABOVE AND BEYOND

Use the **Total Hub Shaper** (pg. 56) to prepare wheels for use with the **Wheel Turning Mandrel** (pg. 53). **Execute these steps before any other wheel preparation technique.**

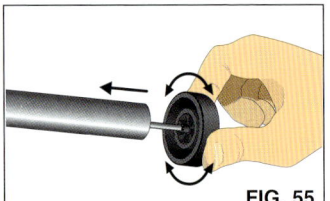
FIG. 55

REAM BORES
Ensure wheels fit properly onto the mandrel by removing mold flash and correcting imperfections inside wheel bores **(Fig. 55)**.

SQUARE INNER HUBS

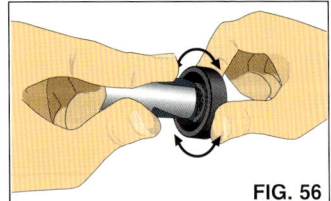
FIG. 56

Ensure equal rotation of wheels by squaring the inner wheel hub to the wheel bore **(Fig. 56)**.

SHAVE OUTER HUBS
Ensure equal rotation of wheels by squaring the outer wheel hub to wheel bore **(Fig. 57)**.

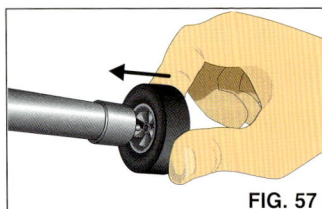
FIG. 57

28

REMOVE BLEMISHES

A **Wheel Turning Mandrel** (pg. 53) is essential for removing wheel blemishes and tuning wheels. Sanding wheels without a wheel mandrel and drill can add defects to the wheel and create an uneven surface.

- Insert the mandrel screw through the back of the wheel hub. Thread it through the wheel gently and into mandrel, then tighten the screw **(Fig. 58)**. The screw should be secure or it could slip as pressure is applied to the wheel, causing damage to the wheel hub. However, do not over tighten and damage wheel hub.
- Clamp drill in a padded vice. Secure mandrel shaft into drill chuck.
- Run drill at low speed. Place medium-grade sandpaper against wheel tread **(Fig. 59)**. Do not apply too much pressure or you may damage the wheel. Sand until blemishes are removed.
- Repeat using fine-grade sandpaper. Sand until the wheel looks smooth.

FIG. 58

FIG. 59

CONE INNER HUBS

Another source of friction is the contact made between the wheel hub and the car body. Coning wheel hubs reduces this contact area and increases car speed. Cone wheels using the **Total Hub Shaper** (pg. 56) or a triangular file.

- When using a triangular file, use the flat side to file a tapered edge around wheel hub **(Fig. 60)**.
- Sand the filed wheel hub with a strip of #400-grit wet/dry polishing paper **(Fig. 61)**. Next, polish the hub with #600 and 1000-grit wet/dry polishing paper. Wipe the wheel hub to remove dust.
- Rub dry graphite on the edge of the filed hub. Tapered wheel hubs should be smooth and rounded **(Fig. 62)**.

FIG. 60

FIG. 61

FIG. 62

POLISH INSIDE RIMS

Another trick for reducing friction is to polish the inside of the wheel rim. The rim may make contact with the center guide rail on the track. If this happens, you want the inside rim of your wheels to be smoothed and polished.

FIG. 63

• With a wheel on the mandrel, run drill at medium speed. Sand the inside of the wheel rim progressively with #400, 600 and then 1000-grit wet/dry polishing paper **(Fig. 63)**. Sand gently so you do not damage the wheel or change its shape.

POLISH BORES

The inside of the wheel bore may be as blemished as the tread. Polishing the bores will give you a smooth, slick surface against your polished axles. Use products from the **Diamond Finishing Kit** (pg. 54) to polish bores **(Fig. 64)**.

FIG. 64

TRICKED-OUT FOR SPEED

Check your official race rules before executing. Wheel modifications are not allowed in a great number of races.

SHAVE WHEELS

Use the **Wheel Lathe** (pg. 56) to remove uneven tread material and ensure wheels are perfectly round and true to the wheel bore.

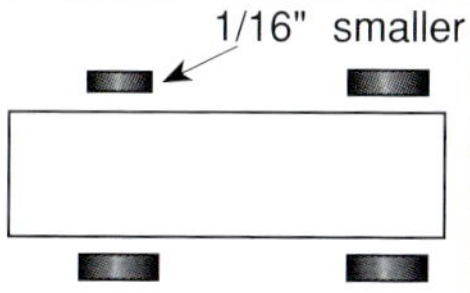

1/16" smaller

FIG. 65

MODIFY WHEELS

Less wheel tread on the track means less friction.

• **Three-Wheel Riding (use the Wheel Lathe)** Make one of your front wheels approximately 1/16" smaller in diameter **(Fig. 65)**. When the smaller wheel is mounted on the racer, it should be completely off the track. Your racer will ride on only three wheels, instead of four.

FIG. 66

For an alternative **Three-Wheel Riding** technique, see page 18.

• **Machined Wheels (requires a lathe machine)** The inertia principle of lathe-turned wheels states, wheels with less mass gain speed faster. Also, reducing the contact area made between

FIG. 67

the wheel the track reduces friction. Examples of wheel modifications **(Fig. 66)**. The wafer wheel **(Fig. 67)** is a modification that eliminates material, rather than reshaping it.

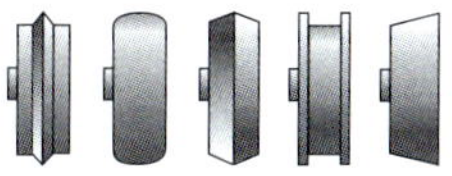

Lubricate

Reduce friction and increase your racer's speed by applying graphite to wheels and axles before attaching them to your racer. Laboratory-tested PineCar lubricants are the highest quality lubricants available.

When using any lubricant, be sure to cover the area where you will be working with newspaper or an old cloth. Lubricants can be very messy. Powdered lubricants are very fine, so be careful when applying. Apply graphite to all wheels and axles.

LUBRICATE WHEELS

- Place a small amount of graphite on a soft cloth. Place the cloth in the palm of your hand. Place the wheel tread on the graphite and turn for even coverage **(Fig. 68)**.

- Place additional graphite on the cloth. Rub the graphite onto the tapered hub.

- Place additional graphite on the cloth. Rub graphite around the inside rim **(Fig. 69)**.

- Place a small amount of graphite on a piece of **Polishing Brush** (included with **Diamond Finishing Kit**, pg. 55). Insert the brush carefully into the wheel bore to lubricate the inside bore.

FIG. 68

FIG. 69

LUBRICATE WHEELS AND AXLES

• Insert axle through front of wheel hub. Apply lubricant on the inside of the wheel hub **(Fig. 70)**, then spin wheel to distribute graphite evenly **(Fig. 71)**.

• On outside of wheel, apply graphite between the wheel and axle head **(Fig. 72)**. Spin wheel to distribute graphite evenly.

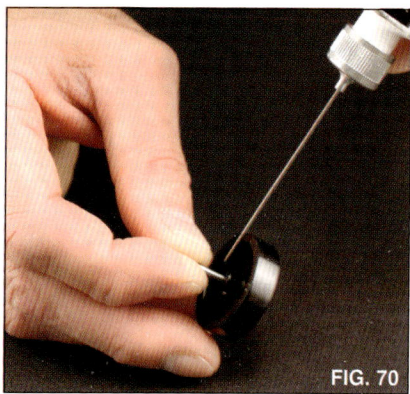

FIG. 70

FIG. 71

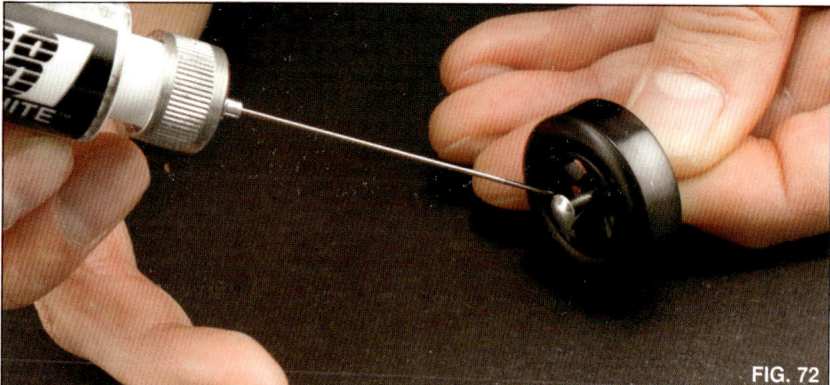

FIG. 72

PINECAR LUBRICANTS

• An excellent lubricant for your racer is **Hob-E-Lube Dry Graphite Lubricant** (pg. 53). It is a finely ground lubricant with Molybdenum. It is safe on all surfaces and easy to use. Molybdenum works like millions of microscopic ball bearings.

• For serious competitors, we recommend **XLR8 Ultra Graphite** (pg. 53). It is laboratory tested for performance and will amp up your racer's speed to the max! The special-blend formula includes a stainless steel needle applicator for precision placement.

• When your derby race prohibits graphite, use **Dry White with Cling** (pg. 53). It is a fine, non-staining lubricant with that clings to smooth surfaces.

Assemble Racer

WEIGH CAR

Weight plays a major role in building a winning racer. To maximize your car's potential energy, make it the maximum weight allowed per race rules. Weigh your car, weights, screws and all the car components before attaching the weights **(Fig. 73)**. Add or deduct weight as needed per official race rules.

Different scales may weigh your racer differently. Even though your scale at home reads exactly 5 ounces, the official race scale could read 5.1 ounces. It is beneficial to be able to adjust your racer's weight easily on race day. We suggest using PineCar **Incremental Weights** and **Tungsten Putty Weight** (pg. 54 and 55).

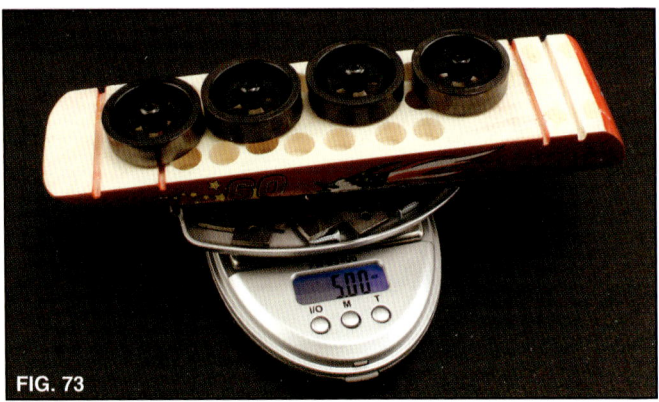

FIG. 73

TEST FIT WEIGHTS

Proper weight distribution will give your car a huge speed advantage. Begin by attaching weights with temporary placement as far to the rear of your racer as possible **(Fig. 74)**. Rear-weighted cars have a center of gravity (CoG) that optimizes performance by maximizing potential energy. Weight placement will be fine-tuned in the next section. Depending on your racer's CoG, weights may need to be moved forward or repositioned.

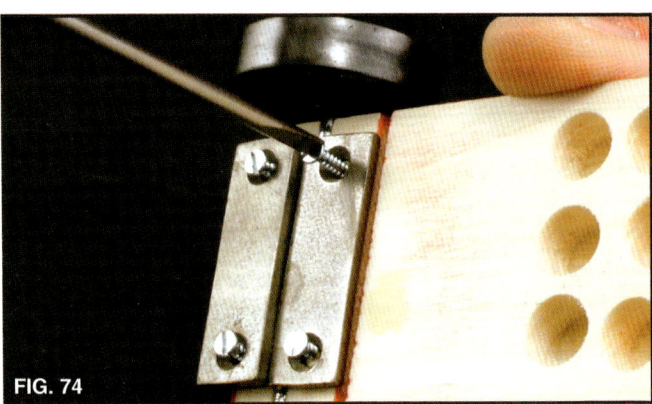

FIG. 74

34

INSTALL WHEELS AND AXLES

Install wheels and axles with a 1/32"–1/16" clearance between the wheels and the racer body **(Fig. 75)**. Use the **Wheel Alignment Tool** (pg. 53) or **Axle Placement Guide** (pg. 56) to measure the clearance or make a spacer from two or three pieces of cardstock **(Fig. 75 inset)**.

NOTE: When surface mounting weights to the bottom of your car, axles must be installed flush with the bottom in order to have a 3/8" clearance between car and track **(Fig. 76)**.

ONE-PIECE AXLES

- Install wheels on one-piece axles **(Fig. 77 inset)**. Lay racer top down on a soft cloth. Center axle over axle slot.
- Tap the axles into place gently with a small hammer **(Fig. 77)**.
- Roll car on a flat surface and make sure the wheels are free-rolling and mounted correctly. If the car pulls left, bend the left side forward and the right side backward **(Fig. 78)**. If your racer pulls to the right, bend the right side forward and the left side backward **(Fig. 79)**. Keep adjusting until your racer runs straight.
- Apply **PineCar Super Glue** (pg. 57) along the length of axle carefully. Be sure to keep adhesive away from the wheels.

NAIL-TYPE AXLES

- Set racer on its side on a soft cloth.
- With a wheel on a nail-type axle, insert the tip of the nail into the front axle slot. Place the Wheel Alignment Tool or a cardstock spacer in between the car body and the wheel hub. Tap the axle/wheel assembly gently into the axle slot with a small hammer **(Fig. 80)**. Repeat procedure to install the rear axle assembly.
- Turn racer over on its other side and place on a wooden block that is covered with a soft cloth. Center the block between the wheels to prevent pressure from being applied to the wheels and axles that are already installed. Install the remaining wheels and axles using the same procedure.
- Check for toe-in/toe-out **(Fig. 81)**. Toe-in or toe-out will slow the speed of your racer. You want your wheels aligned straight and parallel **(Fig. 82)**.
- See **Go Above and Beyond** on page 27 for alternative wheel-mounting methods.

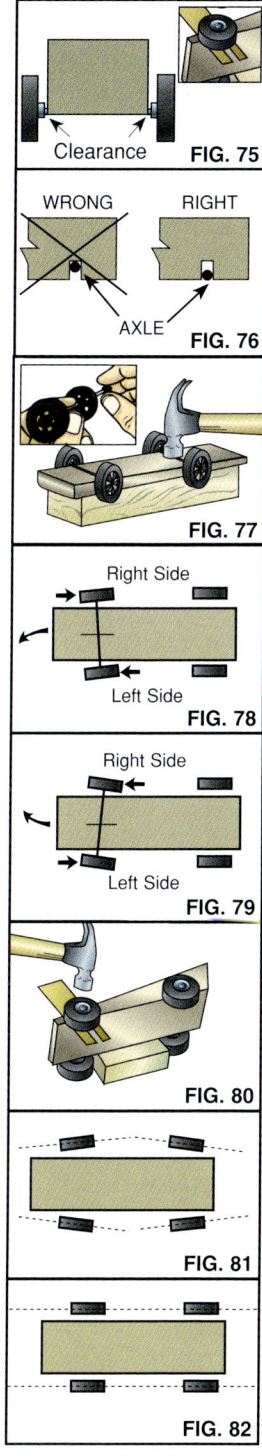

Clearance   FIG. 75

WRONG   RIGHT

AXLE   FIG. 76

FIG. 77

Right Side

Left Side   FIG. 78

Right Side

Left Side   FIG. 79

FIG. 80

FIG. 81

FIG. 82

20-SECOND SPIN TEST

Wheels should spin freely for a minimum of 20 seconds. This test will ensure your wheels and axles are ready to race. Spin and time each wheel individually **(Fig. 83)**. If a wheel does not pass the 20-second spin test, add additional graphite and spin again. If a wheel still falls short, replace the wheel and axle. **NOTE:** Be sure to recheck your car's alignment after installing new wheels and axles.

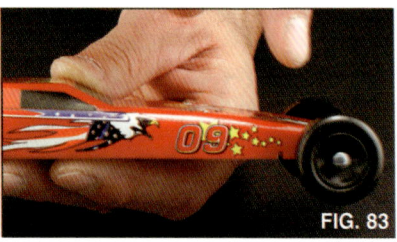

FIG. 83

Make Your Car Race Ready

WEIGHTS AND CENTER OF GRAVITY (COG)

The CoG of a racer is a result of car design and weight placement. Now that weights are in place and wheels are installed, CoG can be measured.

- Measure CoG (balancing point of an object) by placing the car on the edge of a pencil or fulcrum point (included with **CoG System** and **Performance & Conformity System**, pg. 53). Adjust car placement until it no longer rocks back and forth.

FIG. 84

- Measure the distance from the CoG to the rear axles **(Fig. 84)**. It should be approximately 3/4" in front of the rear axles. If the CoG is too far to the rear of your car, it could pop a wheelie or jump the track.

FIG. 85

- If CoG is not in this location, move weights forward or adjust weight configuration and measure again.
- If the CoG is too far forward, remove wood from underneath (pg. 15) and add additional weight toward the rear of the car.
- The **Performance & Conformity System** takes the guesswork out of locating CoG. Simple calculations allow you to determine where to place weights depending on your car's weight and design **(Fig. 85)**.

TEST RUN YOUR RACER

If you have access to a test track, the best way to determine the optimum CoG for your car is do test runs. A finely-tuned CoG will improve your car's speed.
- Begin with a CoG 3/4" in front of the rear axles and test run your racer.
- Move weights slightly forward and test run your car again. Keep adjusting weight placement and configuration, and making test runs. Keep a log of all test-run times.
- When the best time is determined, this is the optimum CoG for your car.

SECURE WEIGHTS

When desired CoG is determined, secure weights to your car **(Fig. 86 & 87)**.

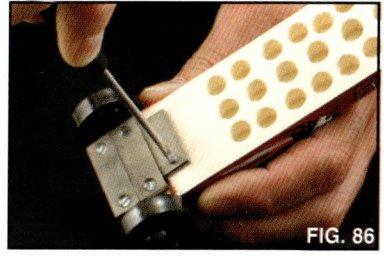

FIG. 86

FIG. 87

VERIFY CONFORMITY

Verify your car meets racing specifications. Using a ruler, **Wheel Alignment Tool** or **Conformity Gauge** (included with **Performance & Conformity System**), confirm your car's measurements per official race rules **(Fig. 88)**.

FIG. 88

BREAK-IN RACER

Break-in your car before race day. Because wheels and axles become smoother with each race, most cars get a little faster each time they make a run down the track. Your car will be faster on the tenth run than it was on the first.

• Apply graphite to wheels and axles, then turn car upright and spin each wheel individually for about 3 minutes **(Fig. 89)**.

• Turn car on its side and spin lower wheels individually for an additional 3 minutes **(Fig. 90)**. Turn car on its other side and repeat. Apply additional graphite periodically.

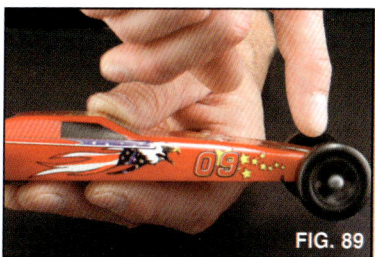

FIG. 89

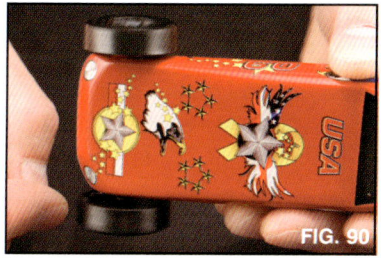

FIG. 90

ADD GRAPHITE BEFORE WEIGH-IN

• The final step in reducing friction is to lubricate wheels and axles before official weigh-in. Apply graphite on the inside of wheel hubs. Spin wheels to evenly distribute graphite.

• Apply graphite between wheel and axle on the outside of each wheel. Spin wheel to evenly distribute graphite.

Race Day!

Race day has finally arrived! We hope you have had a great time building an awesome racer. Here are a few tips to help you have a successful, enjoyable race.

When traveling to your race, be sure to keep your racer protected. You do not want to risk dropping and damaging it. Put in a shoebox or another small box with packing material or foam around it.

Be sure to apply lubricant the before official check-in. If you are allowed to place your own racer on the track, place it straight and centered over the track guide.

OFFICIAL WEIGH-IN

The heavier your racer, the faster it will go! When your car is weighed on the official weigh-in scale, the weight reading may be different from your at-home scale. For this reason, you need to be able to adjust the weight of your car easily on race day. Because it is easier to add weight rather than remove it, have your car a little underweight for weigh-in (check race rules to verify weight can be added on race day).

It is important to take advantage of every ounce of weight available to you per official race rules. If the official weigh-in scale weighs to the nearest 0.1 ounce, cars weighing 4.96 to 5.04 ounces will register 5.0 ounces on the scale. With your racer setting on the official weigh-in scale, place small amount(s) of weight on the scale next to your car until the scale reads 5.1 ounces. Then, remove a tiny amount of weight until it reads 5.0 ounces. Attach the weights to your car.

ADD RACE DAY WEIGHT

Tungsten Putty Weight
• Knead **Tungsten Putty Weight** until pliable and press into predrilled cavity underneath car **(Fig. 91)**.

Adjustable Stick-On Weights
• Attach **Stick-on Weights** with double-sided tape **(Fig. 92)**.
• When attaching weights to the bottom of your racer, make sure there is at least a 3/8" clearance to ensure your car clears the track guide.

FIG. 91

FIG. 92

PineCar Product Listing

PineCar Racer® Basic Kit - P370
Shape and build your own custom racer.

PineCar Racer Wedge Kit - P369
Ready to go. No tools required, just sand, paint and add accessories.

Block - P361
Replacement block for P370.

Wedge - P360
Replacement wedge for P369.

Speed Racer Kit - P3935
Design incorporates aerodynamics, weight distribution and airflow factors.

PRE-CUT DESIGNS™
Rough cut, unfinished shapes. Just sand and paint.

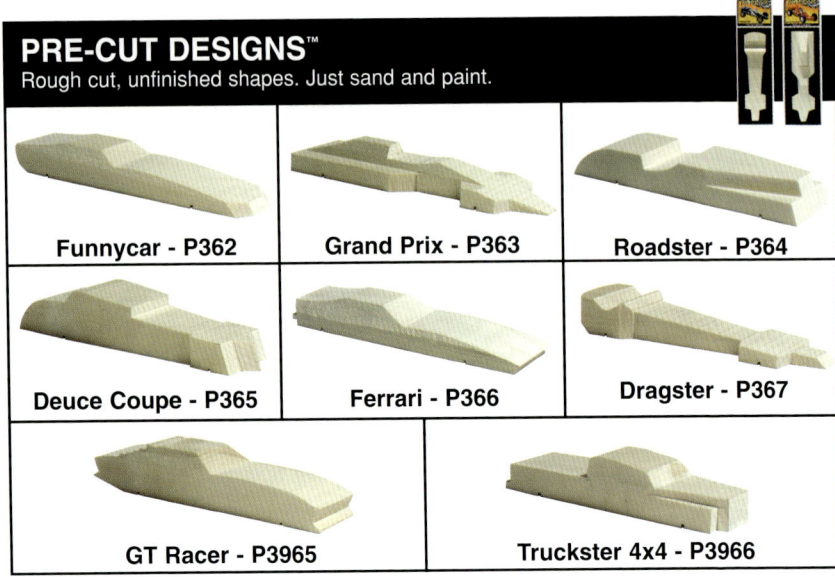

Funnycar - P362

Grand Prix - P363

Roadster - P364

Deuce Coupe - P365

Ferrari - P366

Dragster - P367

GT Racer - P3965

Truckster 4x4 - P3966

AERODYNAMIC PRE-CUT DESIGNS™
Low profile, aerodynamic, rough-cut and ready to finish.

Hammerhead
P3967

Stealth
P3968

White Lightning
P3969

The Blur
P3970

Wafer - P3972

DESIGNER KITS WITH WEDGE
Kits include template, wood wedge, and body parts/details needed to build a racer.

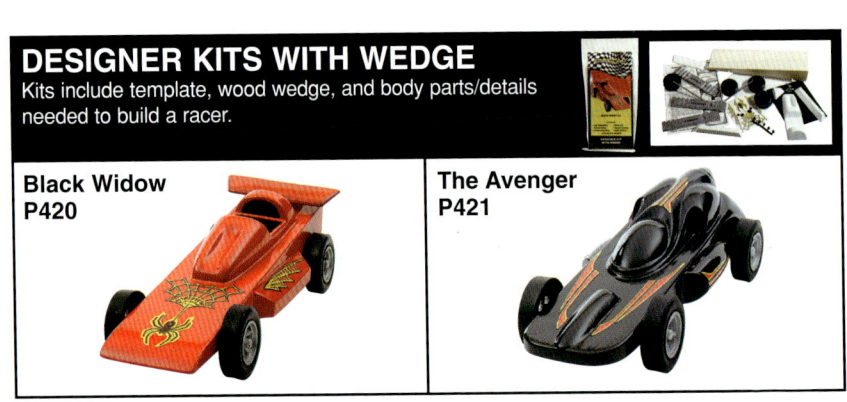

Black Widow
P420

The Avenger
P421

FULL BODY PRE-CUT DESIGNS™

Realistic designs and lightweight. Simply glue, shape, sand and paint.

Tuner Car - P3962

Muscle Car - P3963

Italian Sport - P3964

Stock Car - P3971

4x4 Truck - P3973

American Classic - P3974

CUSTOM BODY KITS

Build the most original car on the track.

Body Builder Kit™ - P4036

Featherweight Customizing Kit™
P3929

DESIGNER KITS

Kits include racer template, prefabricated fenders, Dry Transfer Decals and weights.

Screamin' Eagle
P413

Starfire
P414

Batcar
P415

Thunderbolt
P416

DELUXE CAR KITS

Each kit contains a different pre-cut, unfinished racer body. Includes everything except glue and paint.

 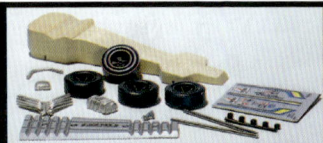

Turbo Funnycar
P371

Formula Grand Prix
P372

Wildfire Roadster
P373

Bandit Coupe
P374

GTS Ferrari
P375

Slingshot Dragster
P376

PINECAR RACER PREMIUM KITS

Complete racer kits that are great for any skill level and require few tools.

Furious Racer
P3945

Baja Racer
P3946

Can Am Racer
P3947

Muscle Racer
P3948

West Coast Growler
P3949

Blue Venom
P3950

STICK-ON DETAILS

Design custom details, cut them out, peel and stick onto your racer.

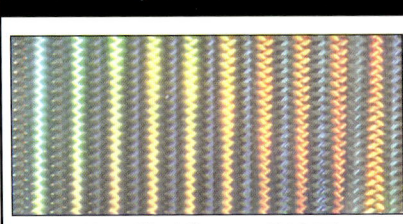

Metallic Mirage - P3987

Black Carbon - P3988

BODY SKIN® CUSTOM TRANSFERS
Use instead of paint or customize a racer with accents and details.

Lightning Strikes
P3975

Smoke Screen
P3976

Fire Starter
P3977

Camouflage
P3978

Gator
P3979

Freedom Flag
P3980

Illusion
P3981

Safari
P3982

Spider Web
P3983

Tie Dye
P3984

Pink Camo
P3985

Psychedelic
P3986

DRY TRANSFER DECALS
The fastest and easiest way to customize your racer.

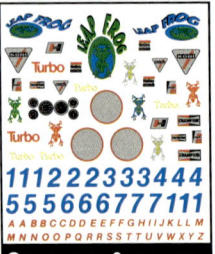

Sponsors & (4" x 5")
Numbers - P306

Drag Racer
P316 (4" x 5")

Dragonfire
P308 (4" x 2½")

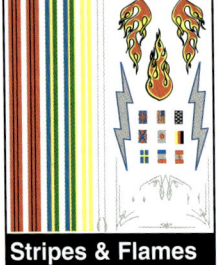

Stripes & Flames
P307 (4" x 5")

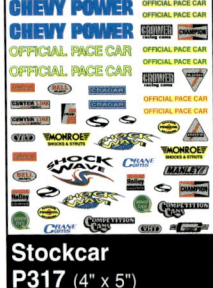

Stockcar
P317 (4" x 5")

Cobra
P309 (4" x 2½")

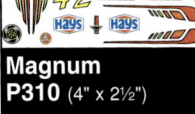

Magnum
P310 (4" x 2½")

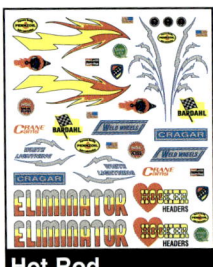

Hot Rod
P314 (4" x 5")

Custom Designs
P318 (4" x 5")

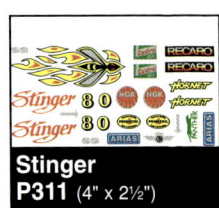

Stinger
P311 (4" x 2½")

Black Widow / Spyder
P312 (4" x 2½")

Off Road
P315 (4" x 5")

Formula
P319 (4" x 5")

Turbo
P313 (4" x 2½")

DRY TRANSFER DECALS
The fastest and easiest way to customize your racer.

Bad to the Bone
P4017 (4" x 5")

Flaming Dragon
P4018 (4" x 5")

Free Bird
P4021 (4" x 5")

Freedom Forever
P4019 (4" x 5")

Rockstar
P4020 (4" x 5")

Peace & Love
P4022 (4" x 2½")

Rockin' Diva
P4023 (4" x 2½")

Wolf
P4027 (4" x 5")

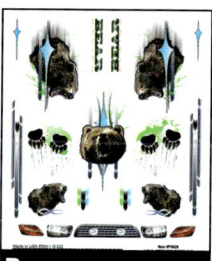

Bear
P4028 (4" x 5")

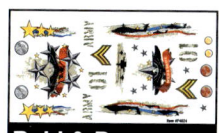

Bold & Brave
P4024 (4" x 2½")

Faith & Honor
P4025 (4" x 2½")

Tiger
P4029 (4" x 5")

Eagle
P4030 (4" x 5")

True Love
P4026 (4" x 2½")

DRY TRANSFER DECALS
The fastest and easiest way to customize your racer.

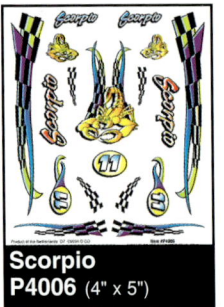

Scorpio
P4006 *(4" x 5")*

Cool Blaze
P4010 *(4" x 5")*

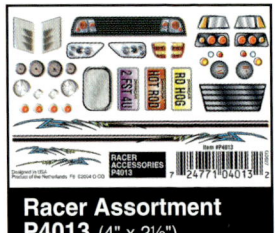

Racer Assortment
P4013 *(4" x 2½")*

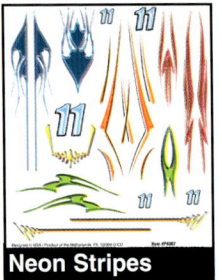

Neon Stripes
P4007 *(4" x 5")*

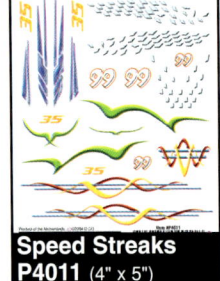

Speed Streaks
P4011 *(4" x 5")*

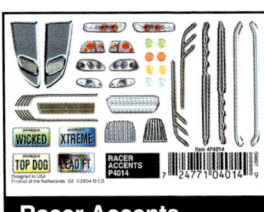

Racer Accents
P4014 *(4" x 2½")*

Blazin' Flames
P4008 *(4" x 5")*

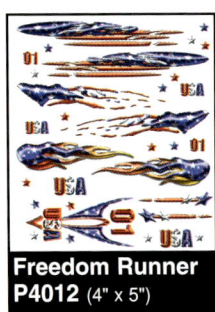

Freedom Runner
P4012 *(4" x 5")*

Beveled Numbers
P4015 *(4" x 2½")*

Yellow Numbers
P4016 *(4" x 2½")*

Drago
P4009 *(4" x 5")*

Racer shown was made using Pre-Cut Design Funnycar (P362) and Dry Transfer Decals Blazin' Flames (P4008).

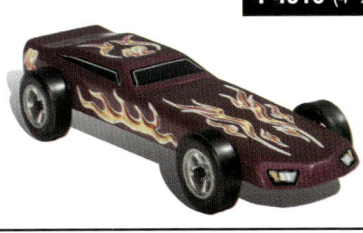

STICK-ON DECALS
Cut out, peel and attach to your racer.

Raptor
P320 (4" x 5")

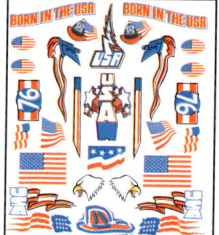

Born in the USA
P462 (4" x 5")

Stars & Stripes
P463 (4" x 5")

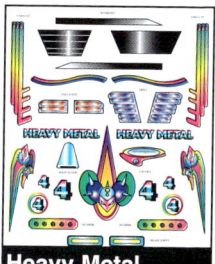

Heavy Metal
P321 (4" x 5")

Magic Machine
P464 (4" x 5")

Captain Zoom
P465 (4" x 5")

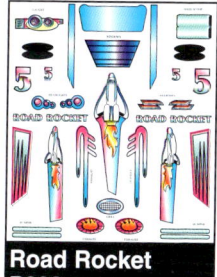

Road Rocket
P322 (4" x 5")

Snake Eyes
P324 (4" x 2½")

Silver Shark
P325 (4" x 2½")

Lightning Rod
P326 (4" x 2½")

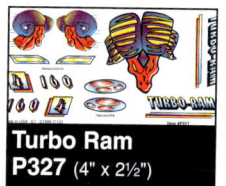

Turbo Ram
P327 (4" x 2½")

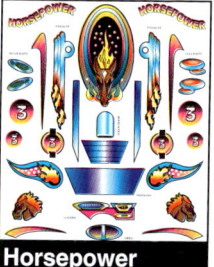

Horsepower
P323 (4" x 5")

*Racer shown
was made using
Pre-Cut Design
(Ferrari P366) and
Stick-On Decals
(Silver Shark P325).*

COMPLETE PAINT SYSTEMS

Everything you need to sand, paint and finish your racer with a high gloss finish.

  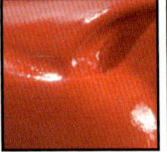  

Cool Blue
P3955

Stealth Black
P3956

Flamin' Red
P3957

Gear Rippin' Green
P3958

Cosmic Yellow
P3959

CUSTOM FINISHING KITS

Use for finishing wood, plastic or metal parts. Includes everything needed to finish any project.

Formula White
P401

Indy Blue
P403

Flame Red
P404

GT Gray
P405

Voodoo Black
P406

Competition Orange - P407

Daytona Blue
P408

Competition Red
P409

Competition Purple - P410

Baja Yellow
P411

Racing Green
P412

SANDING SEALER & WAX

Creates a surface easily sanded to a flawless finish, ready to paint and wax.

WHEEL FLARE® RUB-ON DECALS

Customize derby wheels,
tires and nail heads.

Chrome P4063

Pride P4066

Green Snake P4064

Cyclone P4067

Fire Ball P4065

Juiced P4068

TEMPLATES & STICK-ON DECALS

Each template provides an outline for your racer with decals to add the
finishing touch.

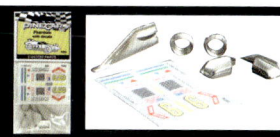

Track Twister - P475

Hot Wings - P476

CUSTOM PARTS WITH DECALS

Engines, pipes, lights, spoilers, roll bars and windshields
transform a simple racer into mean machine. Decals are
an added bonus. Lead-free.

Baja Champ - P330

Drag Star - P331

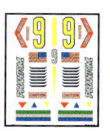

Phantom - P332

Street Rod - P333

CUSTOM PARTS

Drivers, engines, spoilers and roll bars transform a simple racer into an exciting one. Lead-free.

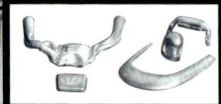

Dune Buster - P340

Eliminator - P341

Star Fire - P342

Formulator - P343

CANOPY, COCKPIT & WINDSHEILD

Canopy & Cockpit Sets - P346
Driver/cockpit set, decals and a canopy top.

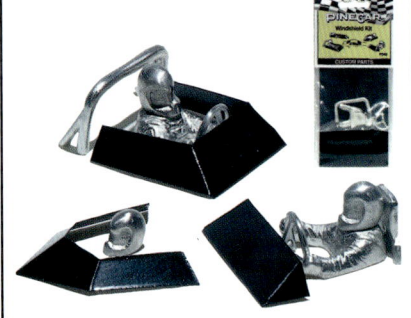

Windshield Kit - P348
Create several windshield designs.

COCKPITS AND DRIVERS

Add humor and character to your racer.

**Mad Racer
P3920**

**Baron Von Gofast
P3921**

SPEED TOOLS

Hob-E-Lube® Dry Graphite Lubricant with Molybdenum - P358

Dry White with Cling - P355

XLR8® Ultra Graphite P4037

Axles & Polishing Kit - P359

Performance & Conformity System™ P4035
Accurately check your car weight, verify racer specifications and locate center of gravity.

CoG System®* - P3918
Distribute weight to achieve optimal center of gravity location and make last minute adjustments.

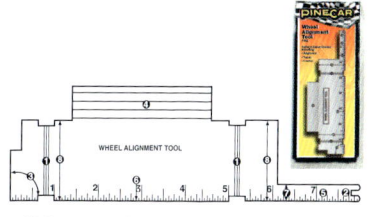

Wheel Alignment Tool - P456
Check wheel alignment, clearance, camber, toe-in, toe-out and other racer specifications.

Wheel Turning Mandrel - P357
Holds wheel secure in drill to remove parting seam and smooth wheel surface.

*Patented Product

53

Diamond Finishing Kit™ - P4039
Specially formulated compound removes the finest axle and hub imperfections and scuffs.

Micro-Polishing System™ - P4038
Progressive polishing system to remove burrs and chamfer, notch and polish axles.

Speed Kit - P356
Includes lubricant, wheel-turning mandrel, axles, polishing materials and weight.

LEAD-FREE INCREMENTAL WEIGHTS

Round P350	Tapered P351	Strip P352	Bar P353

Combo P354	Adjustable Stick-On - P378	Designer Stick-On - P379	Aerodynamic Racer Wt - P326 *non-incremental*

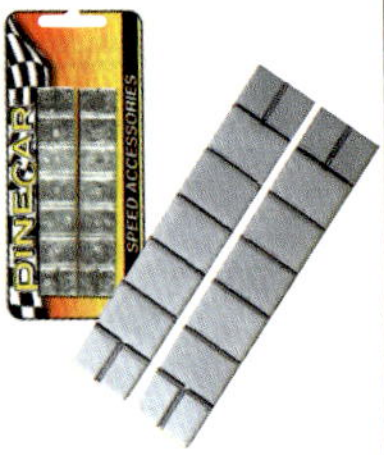

54

LEAD-FREE CHASSIS WEIGHTS™*

4 Wheel Drive
P3910

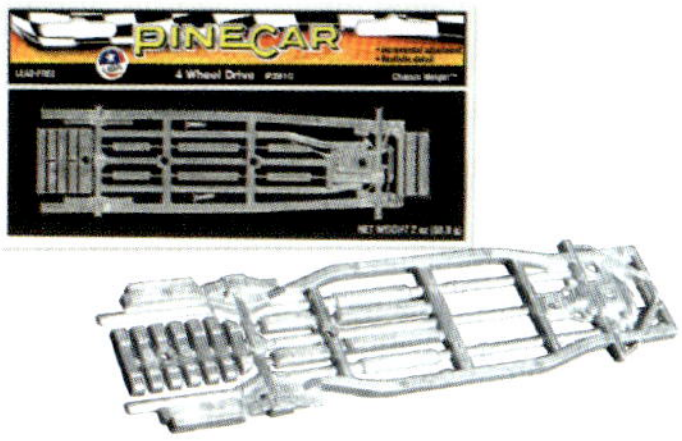

Rear Wheel Drive
P3911

Maximum Torque
P3912

Rocket Car
P3913

TUNGSTEN INCREMENTAL WEIGHTS™

2 oz Cylinder Weights (56.6 g)
P3914

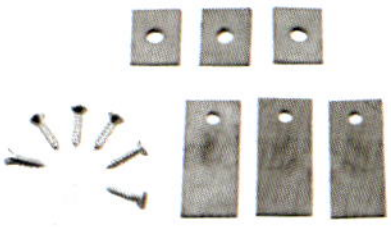

2 oz Plate Weights (56.6 g)
P3916

3 oz Cylinder Weights (85 g)
P3915

3 oz Plate Weights (85 g)
P3917

Tungsten Putty Weight - P3922

EZ-Cut Tungsten Weights™ - P3923

Tungsten CoG Weights™* - P3919

*Patented Product

55

PRECISION TOOLS

High-end tools designed to correct standard manufacturing imperfections of mass-produced car bodies, axles and wheels and for fine-tuning a racer for optimum performance and speed.

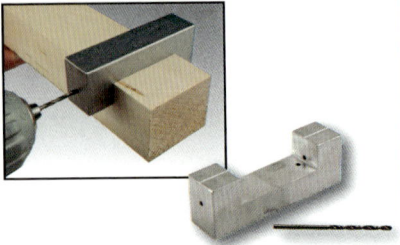

Axle Slot Jig - P4610

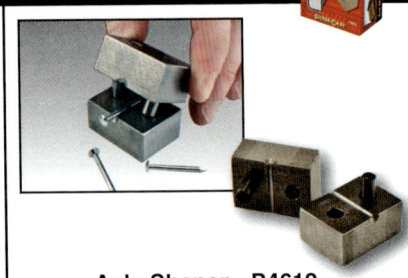

Axle Shaper - P4612

Axle Placement Guide - P4611

Total Hub Shaper - P4614

Straight Tracker - P4613

Wheel Lathe - P4615

TOOLS, ACCESSORIES & ADHESIVES

Racer Shaping Tools - P3930

Rasp and coping saw with five specialty blades for cutting wood and metal.

Body Putty - P3928

Repairs gaps, cuts, or scratches. Great as a smoothing compound.

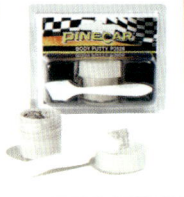

Sanding Pads - P3932

Includes one fine and one medium grade pad. Use wet or dry.

Axle Keepers™ - P458
Keeps axles aligned and securely in place. Maintains adequate track clearance and clear for race day inspection.

Sandpaper Assortment - P380
Quality sandpaper in fine, medium and coarse grades.

Racing Wheels - P347

Show Wheels - P349

5 Axles - P457

Formula Glue® - P384
White glue that is plastic, metal and wood compatible.

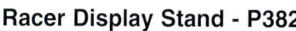

Racer Display Stand - P382

Super Glue - P381
Bonds almost everything to anything instantly.

PINECAR DERBY® RACE PACKAGE* - P459

Package contents
- PineCar Speedway® (32-foot, four-lane track)
- Weigh-In Scale
- Conformity Gauge
- *Program Guide*
- Elimination Charts
- Racing Forms
- Stick-On Number Labels
- Winner Ribbons
- Participant Certificates
- Decorative Racing Pennants

Racers sold separately.
Institutional pricing available.

*Patented Product

SPONSORSHIP ACCESSORIES

PineCar Speedway® - P455
Elimination Charts, Forms and Stickers - P453
Weigh-In Scale and Conformity Gauge - P452
Program Guide - P450
Decorative Racing Pennants (25-feet) **- P429**
Participant Certificates - P425
Participant Ribbons - P426
Winner Ribbons - P427
Race Official/Special Award Ribbons - P428
4" Special Award Trophy - P430
7" Third Place Trophy - P431
8" Second Place Trophy - P432
9" First Place Trophy - P433
10" Deluxe Third Place Trophy - P434
11" Deluxe Second Place Trophy - P435
12" Deluxe First Place Trophy - P436

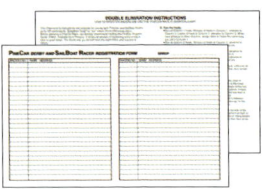

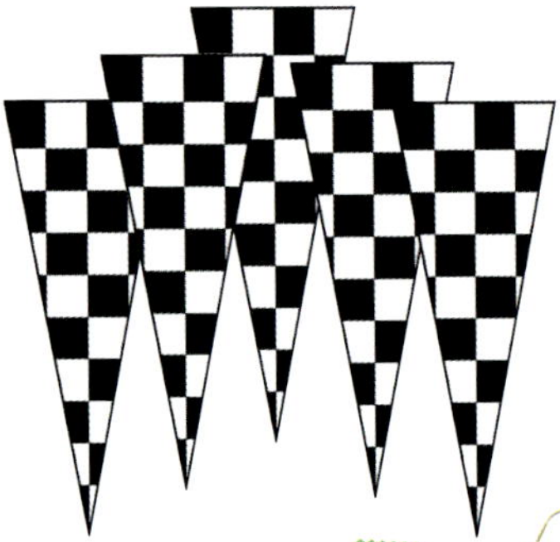

Welcome to Sailboat Racing

WHAT IS SAILBOAT RACING?

SailBoat Racers® are small sailboat models made from a wood hull and mast, plastic sail and rudder and a metal keel. Children can assemble and finish these models with little or no adult assistance. A SailBoat Derby is a fun activity, easily organized and requires very few supplies other than a **SailBoat Racer Kit** (pg. 63). Kids can build and race their boat in the same day!

Races can be held indoors or out, in a swimming pool or using a rain-gutter course. It is an ideal activity for scouts, school projects, youth groups, summer and/or church camps. A SailBoat race would also make a great teambuilding or fundraising event.

The object of the race is to move a boat through a specified course from start to finish by blowing into the sail. If held outdoors, remember that the race would be difficult to hold on a windy day.

Racer shown was made using Body Skin Custom Transfer (Freedom Flag P3980).

SAILBOAT COURSES

There are two types of courses that work well for a SailBoat Derby.

Swimming Pool Course

Set up in the shallow end with a clearly marked point-to-point course or lane(s), avoiding the pool's water jets. For smaller children, a wading pool works well.

Rain Gutter Course

This consists of two 10-foot lengths of rain gutter, arranged side-by-side and set on two sawhorses. The gutters must be level and filled with water to ½-inch from the top.

Racing Procedure

Traditional SailBoat Races are conducted on a single elimination basis. Race participants are divided randomly into heats of two racers. Heat winners are paired against each other in subsequent races until a final winner is declared. Of course, adjustments can be made in racing procedures according to the race organizer's needs, to include number of racers participating in heats and/or creating a double elimination bracket.

Building a Racer

RACING SPECIFICATIONS

1. Hull Length: not longer than 7" or shorter than 6-1/2".

2. Mast Height: 6-1/2" from top to deck.

3. Keel and Rudder: as supplied in SailBoat Racer Kit.

4. Sail: no larger than material supplied in kit.

Building a SailBoat Racer is easy! It takes just five easy steps, and several of the products used to make a PineCar Racer work great on a SailBoat Racer too.

SAND AND SEAL

Sand and seal both the hull and the mast. Sanding Pads (pg. 56) include both the medium and fine-grade needed to sand it smooth. Seal with Sanding Sealer & Wax (pg. 50) or other wood sealer.

PAINT

Complete Paint Systems or **Custom Finishing Kits** (pg. 50) both include everything you need to give your sailboat a smooth, shiny finish. Or, as an alternative to paint and for a customized look, you might want to try **Body Skin Custom Transfers** (pg. 22).

ADD DETAILS

Dry Transfer Decals, **Stick-On Decals** and **Stick-On Details** (pg. 44-49, 63) are the fastest and easiest way to decorate a Sailboat Racer. Choose from a large selection, ranging from colorful, themed original graphics to flames, stripes and numbers.

GLOSS FINISH

You will want to make your SailBoat Racer water resistant to protect the paint. You can use the gloss included in the PineCar paint kits or another water-based gloss finish.

ASSEMBLE

Take a few more minutes to add the keel, mast, rudder and sail and you are ready to sail away!

Keel

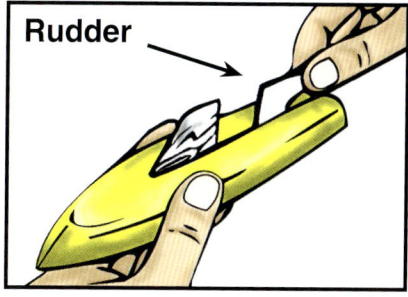

Rudder

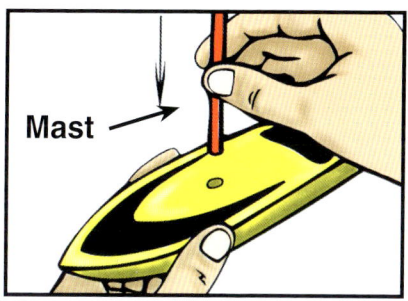

Mast

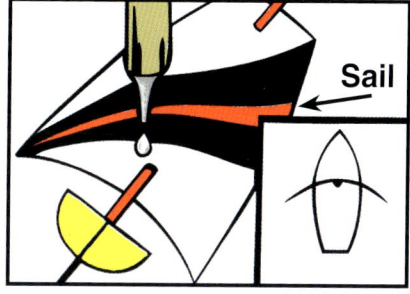

Sail

Race Day!

Here is a suggested set of rules to promote 'fair sailing!' You can of course change them according to your needs.

RULES

1. After the race has begun, participants may not touch their boats.

2. If a race is interrupted by a capsized boat, without interference from another participant, the participant can upright his boat and continue the race. If the same participant capsizes a second time, in the same race without interference, the capsized boat shall be disqualified.

3. If a swimming pool race is interrupted by collision, or interference from another participant (making waves or splashing), the race shall be rerun. If the same participant interferes a second time in the same race, the interfering participant shall be disqualified. If, in the opinion of the judge, the initial interruption was intentional, the interfering participant shall be immediately disqualified.

4. Sailboats that tie will race again.

5. The judge's decision is final.

6. At the start of each race, rain gutter racing participants must hold their sailboats against the back of the rain gutter until the official gives the starting signal. In swimming pool races, participants' backs must be against the side of the pool.

After the race, you can display your Sailboat with the **PineCar Racer Display Stand** (pg. 57).

Sailboat Racer Product Listing

SailBoat Racer Kit - SR470
Includes all the parts needed to build a SailBoat. Paint, glue and decals not included.

SPONSORSHIP ACCESSORIES

Elimination Charts, Forms and Stickers - P453
Decorative Racing Pennants (25-feet) **- P429**
Participant Certificates - SR437
Participant Ribbons - SR438
Winner Ribbons - SR439
Race Official/Special Award Ribbons - SR440
4" Special Award Trophy - SR441
7" Third Place Trophy - SR442
8" Second Place Trophy - SR443
9" First Place Trophy - SR444
10" Deluxe Third Place Trophy - SR445
11" Deluxe Second Place Trophy - SR446
12" Deluxe First Place Trophy - SR447

SAILBOAT RACER DECALS

**Wind Weaver
SR481**
(4" x 5")

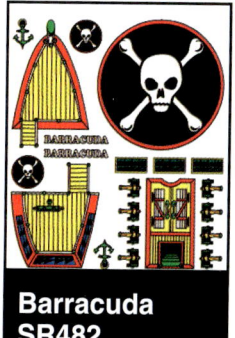

**Barracuda
SR482**
(4" x 5")

**Fittings &
Markings
SR483** (4" x 5")

**Puff
SR484**
(4" x 5")

**Comet
SR485**
(4" x 5")

**Viking
SR486**
(4" x 5")

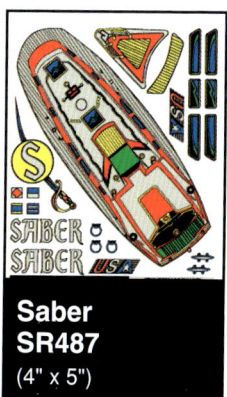

**Saber
SR487**
(4" x 5")

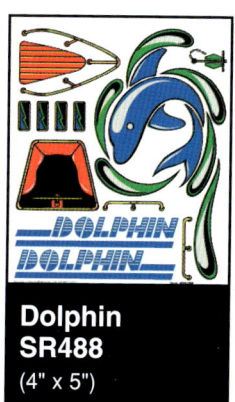

**Dolphin
SR488**
(4" x 5")

INDEX

LEARN HOW TO BUILD AND RACE PINECAR RACERS®

This easy-to-read and complete step-by-step guide helps you build a winning PineCar Racer. Learn the nuts and bolts of designing and building a fast car from a simple wood block. You will also learn simple building and fine-tuning techniques that maximize a car's potential energy and reduce friction. Instructions are easy to follow with plenty of full-color photos and illustrations.

You will begin with the process of designing a racer body, exploring the many options available, depending on your woodworking skill set. Learn how to choose the right type of weight, the best method of fitting it into your design and how to adjust your weight to achieve an optimum center of gravity. Prepare your wheels and axles in a way that reduces friction to a minimum.

Customizing the look of your car is easy, and this book will provide you a range of options, tips and techniques for giving your hot racer the cool look you want.

PineCar is the leading manufacturer of small racecar kits and a full line of supplies. All products are BSA®, Kub Kar™ and RA Racer® compliant when used with approved wheels and axles. Local race rules may vary.

ITEM #P383

PINE

PINECAR® is
PO BOX 98,